THE METROPOLITAN MUSEUM OF ART

Degas
Painter of Ballerinas

SUSAN GOLDMAN RUBIN

Abrams Books for Young Readers

NEW YORK

Library of Congress Cataloging-in-Publication Data

Names: Rubin, Susan Goldman, author.
Title: Degas, painter of ballerinas / Susan Goldman Rubin.
Description: New York: Abrams Books for Young Readers, 2019.
Identifiers: LCCN 2018030053 | ISBN 9781419728433
(hardcover)
Subjects: LCSH: Degas, Edgar, 1834-1917—Juvenile literature. |
Ballet dancers in art—Juvenile literature.
Classification: LCC N6853.D33 R83 2019 | DDC 759.4—dc23

Printed and bound in China
10 9 8 7 6 5 4 3 2 1

Abrams Books for Young Readers are available at special
discounts when purchased in quantity for premiums and
promotions as well as fundraising or educational use. Special
editions can also be created to specification. For details,
contact specialsales@abramsbooks.com or the address below.

Abrams® is a registered trademark of Harry N. Abrams, Inc.

ABRAMS The Art of Books
195 Broadway, New York, NY 10007
abramsbooks.com

OPPOSITE

Two Dancers, Half-length, ca. 1897. In
pastel, Degas caught the dancers as they fixed the
shoulder straps of their bodices. They seem unaware
of the artist closely observing them as they prepare
to go onstage. Degas loved capturing these moments
behind-the-scenes.

As the young girls adjusted their toe shoes and warmed up for class, Edgar Degas studied them. Back at his studio, he made many drawings of the dancers in their silk tights and long gauze skirts. *"People call me the painter of dancing girls,"* he said.

The Dancers, ca. 1900. With pastel and charcoal Degas drew the dancers limbering up and adjusting their ballet slippers as they prepared for class. He composed the sketch on a diagonal, one of his favorite designs.

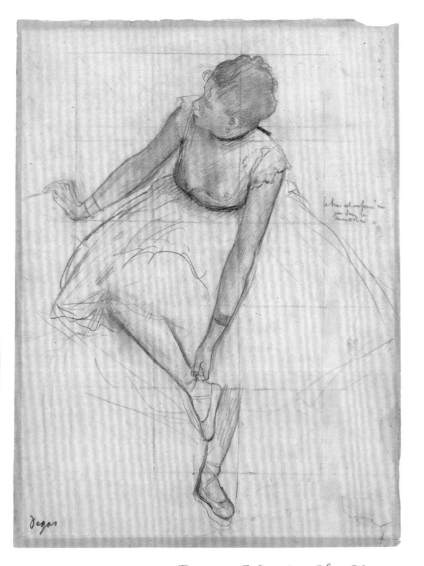

During his long career from 1852 to 1912, Degas created more than a thousand dance pictures. He learned that ballet training was very much like studying art. It took hard work and hours and hours of practice. Degas drew the same poses again and again, just as the dancers repeated their positions at the barre again and again.

"One must repeat the same subject ten times, a hundred times," said Degas. **"Nothing in art, not even movement, must seem an accident."**

Little Girl Practicing at the Bar, ca. 1878–80. The translation of what Degas wrote on this drawing is "battements in second position at the barre." He showed the very young dancer trying hard to achieve the correct position.

His group of fellow artists, the Impressionists, liked painting outdoors. With dabs of color, Claude Monet, a leader of French Impressionism, captured the changing effects of sunlight on the rippling river at a boating resort in *La Grenouillère*.

Not Degas. He spent day after day *indoors*, observing at the Paris Opéra and painting in his studio.

La Grenouillère, 1869, Claude Monet. La Grenouillère (the Frog Pond) was a popular bathing and boating spot on the Seine River near Paris. During the summer, Monet set up his easel in the open air and painted Parisians dining in the floating restaurant, chatting on the little island, and swimming in the river.

4

The Dancing Class, ca. 1870. This was one of Degas's first ballet paintings. In the center, a ballerina named Joséphine Gaujelin waits to do her exercises. A violinist is ready to accompany her.

Young dancers were known as *petits rats*, "little rats," because of their hard life. They were said to be hungry and ready to nibble at anything. The petits rats studied and practiced every day, hoping to become ballerinas and someday earn a living. "Most of them are poor girls doing a very demanding job," said Degas sympathetically.

In class, toe shoes tapped the wooden floor as the girls practiced *rond de jambe*. And *frappé*. And *attitude*. And *arabesque*. Again. And again. And again.

Degas

8

When they stopped to rest, Degas could almost feel how tired they were. He portrayed their gestures: leaning against a bench, stretching, rubbing their aching necks.

Dancer with a Fan, ca. 1880. Degas did this study in pastel and that same year used the figure in a large oil painting, *The Dancing Lesson*. The shape of the dancer's fan repeats the curve of her flared skirt. Degas revealed her exhaustion as she closes her eyes and rubs her neck.

Study of a Ballet Dancer, ca. 1873. For this drawing, Degas experimented with oil mixed with opaque watercolor on bright pink paper and signed his name in red. Degas often drew on tinted papers.

"Bonjour, Monsieur Degas," called the ballet pupils as they scampered into the rehearsal room. He observed the girls rushing up and down the stairs. Later, remembering what he had seen, he made many drawings.

Sometimes the dancers came to his dusty, messy studio. Degas, wearing a long smock over his suit and tie, posed them on platforms set up around the room. "Get used to drawing things from above and below," he reminded himself in his notebook.

Degas understood ballet steps so well that he would often hop around the room mimicking an *arabesque* or a *pirouette*. "It really is funny to see him," said a writer who visited him.

Seated Dancer, 1873–74. Here, Degas added touches of white to his pencil-and-charcoal drawing. He observed that even when a dancer was resting, she held the soles of her feet touching to stretch her thigh muscles and seemed to be memorizing her steps by tracing them with her fingers. The grid he drew enabled him to copy the drawing onto a canvas, and he kept it as part of the picture.

Degas enjoyed talking to the girls and listening to their gossip while they were in his studio. "Degas found them all charming, treated them as if they were his own children, excused everything they did, and laughed at everything they said," recalled another friend.

Degas sketched with his pencil and drew models in the studio, but he waited until he was alone to start a painting in oils. He often combined many of his drawings when he was composing a new painting. He would copy figures from several drawings onto one canvas to create a scene showing a group of dancers. **If the work was going well, he would hum an old tune or sing an aria from one of his favorite operas.**

Two Dancers, ca. 1879. The same girl, Marie van Goethem, posed for these two studies of a dancer adjusting her shoulder strap. Degas did the charcoal drawing on green paper and added highlights with white chalk. Marie also posed for the sculpture *The Little Fourteen-Year-Old Dancer* (see pages 36 and 59).

ometimes Degas invented his own costumes for his paintings. In the classroom, the dancers really wore plain white skirts and tops, but he added blue and pink sashes and black throat ribbons. He needed the accents of color. Once, when Degas was giving art lessons to a friend's son, he told the young student to paint the whole canvas in tones of a single color, perhaps gray or brown. *"You put a little color on it, a touch here, a touch there,"* said Degas, *"and you will see how little it takes to make it come to life."*

Dancer, ca. 1880. Degas added the bright blue sash to this dancer's skirt as a bold accent of color. And he softly smudged touches of blue in her skirt. With charcoal, he created her black velvet neck ribbon, an accessory the dancers never wore in the classroom.

About the time he started painting dancers, Degas began having trouble with his eyesight. He had gone to a doctor and bought a pair of blue-tinted glasses to protect his eyes from sunlight. From that point on, he was frightened that he would go blind.

Two Dancers, 1873. These two dancers busily arrange their bodices. Using a brush, Degas drew them with a sepia (brown pigment) wash and white gouache (opaque watercolor) on pink paper. Later he placed the dancer on the right in his painting *The Dance Class* on pages 18–19. She looks into a mirror. Can you find her?

But Degas forgot to worry about his vision at the Opéra. There he kept observing and drawing the lessons and rehearsals. He sketched the petits rats as they practiced their steps. Occasionally he showed the mothers and big sisters waiting on the sidelines.

Many years later, one of the dancers remembered him fondly as a "quiet, kind old man who wore blue spectacles." Other dancers thought Degas was cranky, interested only in art.

Degas admired the choreographer Jules Perrot and portrayed him in an oil painting, *The Dance Class*. In an earlier version of the painting, he included a watering can, which was used in those days to sprinkle water on the wood floor to lay the dust so that the ballerinas would not slip.

The Dance Class (detail, see full artwork on page 50), 1874. This is the second version of *The Dance Class*, based on Degas's many drawings. It includes the famous dancer and choreographer Jules Perrot. Here, one of the dancers performs an attitude under his watchful eye. Perrot leans on a long stick that he used to thump on the floor to reinforce the tempo of the music. The mirror on the wall reflects the dancers as well as a glimpse of the rooftops of Paris. Degas was fascinated by the contrast between ballet and ordinary life outside.

Degas featured a watering can in another painting, *Dancers Practicing at the Barre*. He gave this one to his friend Henri Rouart. Degas had given Rouart a different picture, a pastel, but took it back to retouch it. Degas reworked the picture so much that he finally confessed that he had "destroyed the work." In exchange, he gave Rouart *Dancers Practicing at the Barre*. Yet Degas was not satisfied with that one either. "Decidedly that watering can is idiotic," he said. "I really must get rid of it."

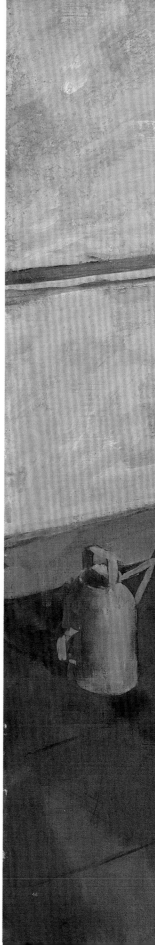

Dancers Practicing at the Barre, 1877. The floor takes up most of this painting. The lines of the wood floor create diagonals like the long barre against the wall. The watering can mimics the movement of the dancer at the right. One critic considered this the finest of all Degas's dance paintings.

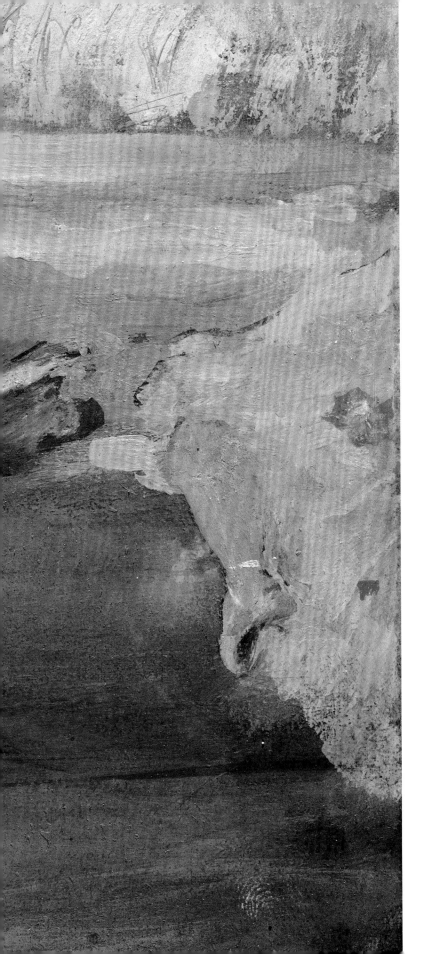

The story goes that Rouart, determined to hold on to his gift, chained *Dancers Practicing at the Barre* to the wall so that Degas could not remove it! Degas "felt a work could never be called *finished*," remembered his friend, the poet Paul Valéry. **Degas was a perfectionist.**

Dancer Onstage (detail, see full artwork on page 53), ca. 1877. Degas gave this picture to Henri Rouart's brother Alexis and his wife.

Degas preferred giving his pictures to friends rather than selling them. Nevertheless, when he needed money, he sold some of his work through his dealers. By the time Degas was fifty, many important collectors competed to buy his ballet paintings and drawings. "When your eyes are trained on those leaping figures, they all come to life," wrote a critic. "You can almost hear the dancing mistress: *'Heels forward . . . hold up your wrists.'*"

The Dance Lesson, ca. 1879. With her leg raised, the dancer waits for the violinist's chord to signal her pirouette. Degas cut the figures off at the frame to create a sense of depth.

n the late 1870s, Degas worked more and more with pastels rather than painting with oils. He loved using the colored chalks because he could combine areas of color with line. With his fingers, he smudged and blended soft tones of blue, white, rose, and green in the skirts of *Three Dancers Preparing for Class*. Then, with a delicate dark line, he picked out details: the shape of one dancer's leg and the legs of her chair, the neck ribbon of another dancer, and the profile of a third arranging her friend's red hair. He described pastel as **"the powder of a butterfly's wings."** He experimented by mixing pastels with charcoal and tempera paint or bleaching his drawings in sunlight to lighten and soften the colors. Sometimes he blew steam over the paper to make the drawing look smeared.

Three Dancers Preparing for Class, after 1878. The dancer seated at center in this pastel is fifteen-year-old Melina Darde. Degas based this picture on studies of Melina and other dancers that he had drawn before.

When Degas was not working in his studio, he went to the Opéra to observe. He still wanted to show the petits rats training to become ballerinas. He admired their dedication. Degas wrote a poem called "Little Dancer" that began:

Dance, winged scamp, dance on the wooden lawns,
Love only that—let dancing be your life.

At age ten or eleven, the girls took an exam. This was the most terrifying day of the whole year for them. They had to perform all alone on an empty stage, accompanied by a pianist. Their teachers, mothers, and the ballet master sat in the front rows of the Opéra, watching. Only the girls who did well were promoted.

Even after years of painting the petits rats, Degas had never attended an exam. When he finally did, he took notes. "It is the age when dancing is pretty," he scribbled. "The jury claps frequently."

Degas noticed everything—he understood the ballerinas' jitters as they got ready to go onstage . . .

Dancers, Pink and Green, ca. 1890. Degas composed this oil painting from many drawings that he had done of moments just before a performance. In the background, blurs of color suggest the scenery. When he worked in oils, he experimented by applying and blending paint with his fingers as well as with his brushes.

Dancer on pointe
(detail, see full artwork
on page 56), ca. 1878.
The ballerina stands en
pointe (on the tip of her
pointe shoe) with her arms
extended. With charcoal,
Degas depicted the flurry
of her movement as she
steps into an arabesque.
Later he used this drawing
for the painting *The Star:
Dancer on Pointe*.

. . . but he
also captured
the thrill of
a successful
performance.

Dancer in Green
(detail, see full artwork on
page 60), ca. 1883. The star
or prima ballerina balances
in an attitude. Her costume
sparkles with pinpoints of
green and flecks of white. In
this pastel, Degas chose the
perspective of looking down
upon the dancer from a box
seat in the Paris Opéra.

During the late 1880s, Degas began to realize that his vision was growing weaker. To save his eyes for artwork, he wrote letters with his eyes half-closed and examined drawings with a magnifying glass.

For his drawings, he used black crayon and charcoal instead of pencil because the marks they made were easier on his eyes. He found it harder to see outlines, so his pastels from this time look fuzzy and abstract. Despite his difficulties, he was eager to work. *"I still dream of projects,"* he wrote.

Dancer with a Fan, ca. 1890–95. Despite his failing eyesight, Degas brings this dancer to life with strong lines of charcoal and smudges of pastel. Color and movement became more important than details such as the face, hands, and shoe ribbons.

On days when Degas could not see well enough to draw or paint, he modeled figures in clay and wax. Using the memory in his fingers, he shaped classic ballet positions, such as *First Arabesque Penché* and *Second Arabesque.*

First Arabesque Penché, modeled probably ca. 1892–96, cast 1920. Using wax, clay, and plastiline, Degas formed a figure in *First Arabesque Penché*. Swooping down with her arms outstretched, she stands on one foot with the other leg raised. Visitors to his studio described him as constantly at work on his wax statuettes in his later years.

These poses were difficult. Once, Degas was sculpting as his model Pauline balanced on one leg while struggling to hold her other foot behind her. Finally she asked for a rest. As Pauline stood near the stove warming herself, she asked Degas to teach her the tune he had just been singing, a minuet from an opera.

"Of course, my girl," he said, "I'll sing it for you." As Degas sang, he made little bows and danced a few steps. And Pauline, laughing, returned the bow. "Degas seemed quite happy," she remembered.

Second Arabesque, modeled probably before 1890, cast 1920. In this sculpture, Degas portrayed another arabesque. The dancer is poised on one leg while her upper body leans forward. Degas was reluctant to finish the sculptures and exhibit them and refused to have them cast in bronze. He would sometimes demolish a statuette after reshaping it, often as many as twenty times, then happily start all over again with a ball of wax.

Around 1880, he started making studies for a small sculpture called *The Little Fourteen-Year-Old Dancer.* Marie van Goethem, a petit rat, was the model. She and her sisters lived near Degas and often posed for him. Degas tinted the wax figure to make it more lifelike. He dressed it in a real bodice, tutu, and ballet slippers and used real hair braided into a pigtail tied with a satin ribbon. When he exhibited the sculpture in 1881, it created a sensation. The wax figure looked so lifelike it startled people and disturbed them. "Simply frightful," declared a critic. "Ugly," wrote a reviewer. But many admired the statue and predicted that it would become a new form of modern art. (And it did!)

The Little Fourteen-Year-Old Dancer (see alternate view on page 59), modeled ca. 1880, cast 1922, tutu 2018. Degas made many drawings of Marie van Goethem from different angles in preparation for modeling this sculpture. Marie stands in open fourth position. This is the only sculpture Degas exhibited in his lifetime. It seems to have been cast in bronze in an edition of twenty-five examples in the 1920s.

Degas did his last dance drawings, *Russian Dancers*, from 1899 to 1905, when he was in his late sixties. The drawings show the dancers merrily kicking up the heels of their red boots.

LEFT

Russian Dancer, 1899. Degas sketched a single dancer in pastel over charcoal on tracing paper. She kicks and swirls in a scene Degas imagined with strokes of blue for sky and green for grass.

OPPOSITE

Russian Dancers, 1899. Degas made vivid pastels of Russian dancers in groups of three. The dancers wear brightly colored skirts and garlands of flowers in their hair. Some scholars say that Degas was inspired by operas that included Russian folk dances. Others think he saw a traveling troupe of dancers in a show and excitedly began his new series.

In his art, Degas captured the joy of dance for all time.

The petits rats live on in his drawings, paintings, and sculptures forever, and even today dancers recognize themselves in his work.

"Drawing," Degas once said, "is not what one sees, but what one can make others see."

The Rehearsal of the Ballet Onstage (detail, see full artwork on page 58), ca. 1874. Degas captured the excitement of a rehearsal at the Paris Opéra in this pen-and-ink drawing covered with a thin layer of oil paint and traces of watercolor and pastel. The ballet master works with the dancers. The scroll of a double bass at the middle foreground indicates the orchestra, a feature Degas used in many paintings.

Edgar Degas

A Brief Biography

Hilaire-Germain-Edgar Degas, one of the greatest artists of the nineteenth century, was born on July 19, 1834, in Paris, France. Edgar was the oldest of five children, three brothers and two sisters. When he was just thirteen his mother died, and his father, Augustin, never remarried.

Edgar adored his young, fun-loving mother and missed her dreadfully, but he soon became used to living in a family dominated by bachelors. Augustin, a distant yet caring father, earned his living as a banker. Nevertheless, he loved art and took Edgar with him to see great paintings at the Musée du Louvre.

Self-Portrait, ca. 1855–56. This is one of forty self-portraits Degas produced in various media. Here, he painted a likeness of himself in oil on paper that he laid down on canvas. At the time of this painting, Degas was in his early twenties and had quit his formal training at the École des Beaux-Arts and set off to travel in Italy.

At age twelve, Edgar went to boarding school in Paris and, like many of his classmates, took extra lessons in drawing once a week. When he was nineteen he entered law school, to please his father. But Edgar did not want to be a lawyer. *"I want to be a painter!"* he announced. His father was horrified—being an artist was no way to earn a living. Edgar moved into a miserable attic to prove that he meant what he said. His father relented and gave his approval of his son's new career.

Edgar Degas began his training by copying works of the great masters that hung in the Louvre and in the Musée du Luxembourg, the world's first museum of contemporary art. His idol was the artist Jean-Auguste-Dominique Ingres. Once Degas met Ingres, who told him, "Draw lines, young man, lots of lines, either from memory or from nature." Degas took this advice and became an outstanding draftsman.

At age twenty, Degas briefly attended École des Beaux-Arts (School of Fine Arts), but he dropped out and studied privately with professors of art. During this period, he made many drawings and paintings of his sisters and brothers, as well as self-portraits. In the summer of 1856, he went to Naples, Italy, his father's birthplace, and stayed at his

The Bellelli Family, 1858–1867. Degas painted this portrait in Paris, but he based it on studies he made in Florence when he visited his beloved aunt Laura Bellelli. She is shown standing between her daughters. Her husband, Baron Bellelli, seated on the right, is partly turned away as he works at his desk. Degas sympathetically depicted the distance between his aunt and her husband, to whom she was unhappily married.

grandfather's huge villa. While there, Degas sketched and painted pictures of his relatives. His studies of his favorite aunt, Laura, later evolved into one of his masterpieces, *The Bellelli Family*, depicting her and her husband and daughters. After three years in Italy, Degas returned to Paris and began a series of paintings depicting historical scenes. Then, in 1865, he turned once again to doing portraits. About this time, he became interested in painting scenes of contemporary life around him—theater, concerts, and horse races. At the racetrack, he sketched the spectators as well as the jockeys on horseback. In his studio, Degas modeled small sculptures of horses to help him understand the figures in three dimensions.

Three Jockeys, ca. 1900. Horses and riders, like dancers, attracted Degas as subjects for his art. He captured the way jockeys sat on racehorses, leaning forward, handling the reins. In this pastel, Degas humorously shows the horse on the left extending its neck to graze, which racehorses were trained not to do.

Around 1867, when he was thirty-three years old, he made his first ballet painting, *Portrait of Mlle Fiocre in the Ballet "La Source."* It was based on a real ballet, a fairy tale that featured a live horse on the stage! Degas put the horse in his painting. During the next few years, he did more paintings of ballet performances, and by the early 1870s, Degas had started to go behind the scenes at the Paris Opéra.

Degas had been working hard at his art for many years, and he needed a rest. In 1872, he traveled to the United States for a visit to New Orleans, Louisiana, where his mother had been born. His brothers, René and Achille, lived there and were business partners. René had started out working in their uncle's cotton business. At first, Degas loved New Orleans. *"Everything attracts me here,"* he wrote. He began a large picture of his family's office, *A Cotton Market in New Orleans*, which included portraits of his uncle and two brothers. But he finished the painting in Paris, for after a few months of traveling, Degas felt homesick. He especially missed the opera and ballet and wanted to be back in time for a performance by one of his favorite dancers.

The artists' community in Paris was brimming with new ideas. Degas and other modern French artists had recently seen prints from Japan—full of unusual viewpoints and strange angles—for the first time. The prints inspired Degas with fresh ideas for composition.

Photographs influenced him, too. Degas became excited about the new process of photography, first introduced around 1848, and he experimented with his own camera.

A Cotton Market in New Orleans, 1873. Degas interrupted his dance pictures to visit his brothers and other relatives in New Orleans, Louisiana. His uncle Michel Musson, a textile manufacturer, is seated in the foreground, examining cotton samples that have just arrived. Degas's brother René sits behind him, reading the local newspaper. On the far left, Degas's brother Achille leans against a windowsill. Degas had loaned money to his brothers to help them establish a wine-importing business in the city.

[Self-Portrait in Library (Hand to Chin)], ca. 1895. Degas made this self-portrait with a camera when he was sixty-one. He became passionate about photography in the 1880s and 1890s. Often his friends posed for him, and he carefully composed the photographs telling the models what to do and where to look. He especially cared about lighting and capturing night effects as he did in this self-portrait.

He also continued to sculpt figures in clay and wax.

Degas often used ordinary women as his models. From dancers and singers to laundresses and shopgirls, Degas portrayed women at work. His circle of friends included female artists such as Berthe Morisot and Mary Cassatt. Yet he never married and had no children. *"I was in love with art,"* he once said.

Degas lived alone and was looked after by a housekeeper. He fussed constantly about his health, and though he enjoyed delicious food, he told his housekeeper to cook plain meals because he believed that diet was good for him. Even his close friends thought he was a worrywart. They knew he had odd habits. When invited to a dinner party, Degas gave his host strict instructions: No flowers on the table. No cats or dogs in the dining room. No perfume on the women. "And very few lights," he said.

As a young man, Degas began having trouble with his eyes, and his condition kept growing worse. At the end of his life, he was almost blind. He would run his hand along his paintings to feel the smooth texture. He would praise a picture by saying, "It's flat like good paintings." Degas was referring to the old masters' paintings in the Louvre that were finished with a thin coat of varnish that made them smooth. He had adopted the same technique.

In 1912, when he was seventy-eight, Degas stopped working altogether and spent his time strolling alone through the streets of his beloved Paris. "My legs are good. I walk well," he said. Nonetheless, Degas used a cane. And his eyesight was probably just clear enough to let him see curbs and cross streets by himself.

In the last year of his life, Degas became ill and had to stay in bed. He died in 1917. His tombstone reads, "He loved drawing very much."

AUTHOR'S NOTE

I was elated when my editor, Howard Reeves, asked me to write a book about Edgar Degas and his drawings, paintings, and sculptures of dancers. The project would be in collaboration with The Metropolitan Museum of Art. As a girl growing up in New York, I began studying art when I was ten, and was frequently taken to The Met before I could go there by myself. Because I also loved ballet, Degas's pictures of ballerinas were my favorites. I was in awe of his exquisite draftsmanship and his gorgeous colors. The dancers practicing their steps, and the small bronze sculptures caught in the midst of movement, almost leaped to life. While researching this book, I was fascinated to discover the stories behind the artworks. And now it is a pleasure to present Degas's art of the dance to young readers.

The Dance Class, 1874.

SEE DETAIL, PAGES 18-19

NOTES

PAGE 1 "People call . . . dancing girls." Richard Kendall, ed., *DEGAS by himself: Drawings, Prints, Paintings, Writings* (Boston: Little, Brown, 1987) 306.

PAGE 3 "One must . . . seem an accident." Lillian Schacherl, *Edgar Degas: Dancers and Nudes* (Munich and New York: Prestel, 1997) 18.

PAGE 7 "Most of . . . demanding job." Kendall, *DEGAS by himself*, 314.

PAGE 10 "Bonjour, Monsieur Degas." Lillian Browse, *Degas Dancers*. (New York: Studio Publications, 1948), 68.

PAGE 10 "Get used . . . and below." Kendall, *DEGAS by himself*, 113.

PAGE 10 "It really is . . . see him." Carol Armstrong and David Hockney (postscript), *A Degas Sketchbook* (Los Angeles: Getty Trust Publications, 2000) 38.

PAGE 13 "Degas found . . . everything they said." Roy McMullen, *Degas: His Life, Times, and Work* (Boston: Houghton Mifflin, 1984) 267.

PAGE 14 "You put . . . come to life." Daniel Halévy, *My Friend Degas* (Middletown, CT: Wesleyan University Press, 1964) 67.

PAGE 18 "quiet, kind . . . blue spectacles." Denys Sutton, *Degas: Life and Work* (New York: Abbeville Press, 1991) 202.

PAGE 20 "destroyed the work." McMullen, *Degas*, 363–364

PAGE 20 "Decidedly that . . . rid of it." Ibid., 363–364.

PAGE 23 "felt . . . called *finished*." Paul Valéry, *Degas, Manet, Morisot* (Princeton, NJ: Princeton University Press, 1960) 50.

PAGE 25 "When your . . . up your wrists." Henri Loyrette, *Degas: The Man and His Art* (New York: Harry N. Abrams, 1993) 66.

PAGE 26 "the powder of butterfly's wings." Ibid., 77.

PAGE 29 "Dance, winged . . . be your life." Robert Gordon and Andrew Forge, *Degas* (London: Thames and Hudson, 1988) 204.

PAGE 29 "It is . . . claps frequently." Kendall, *DEGAS by himself*, 105.

PAGE 32 "I still dream of projects." Malcolm Forbes, "Degas: a passion for perfection," *The National*, December 20, 2017, 3 of 9.

PAGE 35 "Of course . . . for you . . . happy." Gordon and Forge, *Degas*, 210.

PAGE 37 "Simply frightful." Richard Kendall, *Degas and the Little Dancer* (New Haven, CT: Yale University Press, 1998) 43.

PAGE 37 "Ugly." Ibid., 45.

PAGE 40 "Drawing . . . make others see." Ibid., 319.

PAGE 43 "I want to be a painter!" McMullen, *Degas*, 31.

PAGE 44 "Draw lines . . . from nature." Ibid., 37.

PAGE 46 "Everything attracts me here." Susan E. Meyer, *Edgar Degas* (New York: Harry N. Abrams, 1994) 37.

PAGE 48 "I was in love with art." Forbes, "Degas: a passion for perfection," 3 of 9.

PAGE 49 "And very few lights." Kendall, *Degas and the Little Dancer*, 305.

PAGE 49 "It's flat like good paintings." Gordon and Forge, *Degas*, 271.

PAGE 49 "My legs . . . walk well." Halévy, *My Friend*, 110.

PAGE 49 "He loved drawing very much." Schacherl, *Edgar Degas*, 121.

GLOSSARY

Art Terms

charcoal A black material made of carbon that is used for drawing.

composition An arrangement of the parts of a picture.

crayon A stick of colored wax, charcoal, or chalk.

dealers Representatives of artists who show and sell their work, often in galleries.

drawings Pictures made with pencil, pen, crayon, or chalk, usually on paper.

École des Beaux-Arts The School of Fine Arts in Paris, the most important art school in France.

Impressionists Nineteenth-century artists who painted with short brushstrokes and pure color to depict the changing effects of light in scenes of everyday life.

masterpieces Artistic works of extraordinary skill.

modeled Shaped by the artist's hands.

models People who pose for an artist.

modern art Works produced approximately from the mid-nineteenth to mid-twentieth century by artists who put aside traditional subjects and techniques of the past to experiment with new styles of painting and sculpting.

Musée du Louvre A palace in Paris that was turned into a national art museum—the largest art museum in the world.

Musée du Luxembourg A Paris art museum that in the early nineteenth century was the first to show the work of living artists.

oils Slow-drying paints made of pigments combined with linseed oil.

paintings Pictures made with coloring matter (paint) on a flat surface, such as canvas.

pastels Round or square sticks of powdered pigment, a coloring substance.

pencil A slender tube of wood or metal containing graphite, a mineral.

sculpting Carving or shaping a form out of a material like wood, stone, or clay.

self-portraits Pictures that artists draw or paint of themselves.

studio An artist's workroom.

tempera A fast drying paint mixed with water.

Ballet Terms

arabesque   Standing on one leg with the other leg extended behind the body in a straight line.

attitude   Standing on one leg with the other leg lifted in front or back with the knee bent.

barre   A horizontal bar—usually made of wood—along a studio wall for class exercises.

choreographer   A person who plans the steps and patterns of a ballet or dance.

frappé   At the barre, extending the leg, pointing the foot, and striking the floor in front, to the side, in back, and finishing in first position.

pirouette   A complete spin of the body while balancing on one foot.

positions   In classical ballet the five basic ways of placing feet flat on the floor:

first position   Heels are together with toes facing out.

second position   Feet are apart pointing out in opposite directions.

third position   The heel of one foot is placed against the arch of the other.

fourth position   One foot is placed in front of the other, like the pose of *The Little Fourteen-Year-Old Dancer*.

fifth position   The heel of one foot is pressed against the toe of the other to form two parallel lines.

rond de jambe   Starting in first position, making a half circle with the leg from front to side to back, or, beginning in the back, moving the leg to the side, then front, and to first position.

WHERE TO SEE ARTWORKS BY EDGAR DEGAS

United States

CALIFORNIA
Fine Arts Museums of San Francisco
Hammer Museum, Los Angeles
J. Paul Getty Museum, Los Angeles
Los Angeles County Museum of Art
Norton Simon Museum, Pasadena
San Diego Museum of Art

CONNECTICUT
Hill-Stead Museum, Farmington
Yale University Art Gallery, New Haven

ILLINOIS
Art Institute of Chicago
Smart Museum of Art at University of Chicago

INDIANA
David Owsley Museum of Art at Ball State University, Muncie
Indianapolis Museum of Art

IOWA
University of Iowa Stanley Museum of Art, Iowa City

MAINE
Bowdoin College Museum of Art, Brunswick
Davistown Museum, Liberty
Portland Museum of Art

MARYLAND
Walters Art Museum, Baltimore

MASSACHUSETTS
Clark Art Institute, Williamstown
Harvard Art Museums, Cambridge
Museum of Fine Arts, Boston

MICHIGAN
Detroit Institute of Arts

MINNESOTA
Minneapolis Institute of Art

MISSOURI
Mildred Lane Kemper Art Museum at Washington University in St. Louis

NEBRASKA
Joslyn Art Museum, Omaha

NEW HAMPSHIRE
Currier Museum of Art, Manchester

NEW JERSEY
Princeton University Art Museum, Princeton

NEW YORK
Brooklyn Museum, New York City
Frick Collection, New York City
Hyde Collection, Glens Falls
Memorial Art Gallery at University of Rochester
The Metropolitan Museum of Art, New York City
Museum of Modern Art, New York City
Pierpont Morgan Library & Museum, New York City
Solomon R. Guggenheim Museum, New York City

NORTH CAROLINA
Ackland Art Museum at University of North Carolina at Chapel Hill
North Carolina Museum of Art, Raleigh

OHIO
Cincinnati Art Museum
Cleveland Museum of Art
Toledo Museum of Art

OKLAHOMA

Fred Jones Jr. Museum of Art at University of
Oklahoma, Norman

PENNSYLVANIA

Arthur Ross Gallery at University of Pennsylvania,
Philadelphia

Philadelphia Museum of Art

Reading Public Museum

RHODE ISLAND

Rhode Island School of Design Museum, Providence

TENNESSEE

Dixon Gallery and Gardens, Memphis

TEXAS

Blanton Museum of Art at University of Texas, Austin

Dallas Museum of Art

Kimbell Art Museum, Fort Worth

Museum of Fine Arts, Houston

Nasher Sculpture Center, Dallas

VIRGINIA

Chrysler Museum of Art, Norfolk

Virginia Museum of Fine Arts, Richmond

WASHINGTON, D.C.

Hirshhorn Museum and Sculpture Garden

National Gallery of Art

WISCONSIN

Milwaukee Art Museum

Australia

National Gallery of Australia, Canberra

National Gallery of Victoria

Queensland Art Gallery, Brisbane

Canada

Art Gallery of Ontario, Toronto

MacKenzie Art Gallery, Regina

National Gallery of Canada, Ottawa

France

Fondation Bemberg Musée, Toulouse

Musée des Beaux-Arts de Lyon

Musée des Beaux-Arts de Tours

Musée d'Orsay, Paris

Musée du Louvre, Paris

Réunion des Musées Nationaux, Paris

Ireland

Dublin City Gallery The Hugh Lane

New Zealand

Christchurch Art Gallery Te Puna o Waiwhetu

United Kingdom

ENGLAND

Barber Institute of Fine Arts, Birmingham

Birmingham Museum and Art Gallery

British Museum, London

Courtauld Institute of Art, London

Fitzwilliam Museum at University of Cambridge

National Gallery, London

National Museums Liverpool

New Art Gallery Walsall

Southampton City Art Gallery

Tate Gallery, London

Victoria and Albert Museum, London

Whitworth Art Gallery at University of Manchester

SCOTLAND

Glasgow Museums

Scotland National Gallery, Edinburgh

WALES

Amgueddfa Cymru—National Museum Wales,
Cardiff

BIBLIOGRAPHY

*Denotes works suitable for young readers.

Works on Degas

*Armstrong, Carol and David Hockney (postscript). *A Degas Sketchbook*. Los Angeles: Getty Trust Publications, 2000.

Boggs, Jean Sutherland. *Degas*. New York: The Metropolitan Museum of Art, and Ottawa: National Gallery of Canada, 1988.

Browse, Lillian. *Degas Dancers*. New York: Studio Publications, 1948.

DeVonyar, Jill and Richard Kendall. *Degas and the Dance*. New York: Abrams, 2002.

Forbes, Malcolm. "Degas: a passion for perfection." *The National*, December 20, 2017. Also available at: www.thenational.ae/arts-culture/art /degas-a-passion-for-perfection-1.689026.

Gordon, Robert, and Andrew Forge. *Degas*. New York: Harry N. Abrams, 1988.

*Halévy, Daniel. *My Friend Degas*. Middletown, CT: Wesleyan University Press, 1964.

Kendall, Richard. *Degas and the Little Dancer*. New Haven, CT: Yale University Press, 1998.

*Kendall, Richard, ed. *DEGAS by himself: Drawings, Prints, Paintings, Writings*. Boston: Little, Brown, 1987.

Loyrette, Henry. *Degas: The Man and His Art*. Discoveries series. New York: Harry N. Abrams, 1993.

McMullen, Roy. *Degas: His Life, Times, and Work*. Boston: Houghton Mifflin, 1984.

*Meyer, Susan E. *Edgar Degas*. First Impressions series. New York: Harry N. Abrams, 1994.

Schacherl, Lillian. *Edgar Degas: Dancers and Nudes*. Munich and New York: Prestel, 1997.

Sutton, Denys. *Degas: Life and Work*. New York: Abbeville Press, 1991.

*Valéry, Paul. *Degas, Manet, Morisot*. Princeton, NJ: Princeton University Press, 1960.

Works on Ballet

Gresovic, Robert. *Ballet 101*. New York: Hyperion, 1998.

*Kirstein, Lincoln. *The Classic Ballet: Basic Technique and Terminology*. New York: Alfred A. Knopf, 1952, and Gainesville, FL: University Press of Florida, 1998.

———. *Dance: A Short History of Classic Theatrical Dancing*. Trenton, NJ: Princeton Book Company, 1987.

———. *Four Centuries of Ballet: Fifty Masterworks*. New York: Dover, 1984.

Dancer on pointe, ca. 1878.
SEE DETAIL, PAGE 30

LIST OF ILLUSTRATIONS

All artworks from The Metropolitan Museum of Art unless otherwise noted.

PAGE 34 *First Arabesque Penché*, modeled probably ca. 1892–96, cast 1920, Edgar Degas (French, Paris 1834–1917 Paris). Bronze. 17¼ × 21½ × 9⅝ in (43.8 × 54.6 × 24.4 cm). H.O. Havemeyer Collection, Bequest of Mrs. H.O. Havemeyer, 1929. 29.100.390.

PAGE 35 *Second Arabesque*, modeled probably before 1890, cast 1920, Edgar Degas (French, Paris 1834–1917 Paris). Bronze. 11⅜ × 17⅛ × 3⅞ in (28.9 × 43.5 × 9.8 cm). H.O. Havemeyer Collection, Bequest of Mrs. H.O. Havemeyer, 1929. 29.100.399.

PAGES 36, 59 *The Little Fourteen-Year-Old Dancer*, modeled ca. 1880, cast 1922, tutu 2018, Edgar Degas (French, Paris 1834–1917 Paris). Partially tinted bronze, cotton tarlatan, silk satin, and wood. 38½ × 17¼ × 14⅜ in (97.8 × 43.8 × 36.5 cm). H.O. Havemeyer Collection, Bequest of Mrs. H.O. Havemeyer, 1929. 29.100.370.

PAGE 38 *Russian Dancer*, 1899, Edgar Degas (French, Paris 1834–1917 Paris). Pastel over charcoal on tracing paper. 24⅜ × 18 in (61.9 × 45.7 cm). H.O. Havemeyer Collection, Bequest of Mrs. H.O. Havemeyer, 1929. 29.100.556.

PAGE 39 *Russian Dancers*, 1899, Edgar Degas (French, Paris 1834–1917 Paris). Charcoal and pastel, on tracing paper, mounted on cardboard. 24¾ × 25½ in (62.9 × 64.8 cm). Robert Lehman Collection, 1975. 1975.1.166.

PAGES 40–41, ABOVE, FRONT COVER *The Rehearsal of the Ballet Onstage*, ca. 1874, Edgar Degas (French, Paris 1834–1917 Paris). Oil colors freely mixed with turpentine, with traces of watercolor and pastel over pen-and-ink drawing on cream-colored wove paper, laid down on bristol board and mounted on canvas. 21⅜ × 28¾ in (54.3 × 73 cm). H.O. Havemeyer Collection, Gift of Horace Havemeyer, 1929. 29.160.26.

PAGE 42 *Self-Portrait*, ca. 1855–56, Edgar Degas (French, Paris 1834–1917 Paris). Oil on paper, laid down on canvas. 16 × 13½ in (40.6 × 34.3 cm). Bequest of Stephen C. Clark, 1960. 61.101.6.

PAGE 44 *The Bellelli Family*, 1858-1867, Edgar Degas (French, Paris 1834–1917 Paris). Oil on canvas. 78¾ × 98¼ in (201 × 249.5 cm). Musée d'Orsay, Paris, France. RF 2210.

PAGE 45 *Three Jockeys*, ca. 1900, Edgar Degas (French, Paris 1834–1917 Paris). Pastel on tracing paper, laid down on board. 19¼ × 24½ in (48.9 × 62.2 cm). Partial and Promised Gift of Mr. and Mrs. Douglas Dillon, 1992. 1992.103.1.

PAGE 47 *A Cotton Market in New Orleans*, 1873, Edgar Degas (French, Paris 1834–1917 Paris). Oil on canvas. 29 × 36 in (73 × 92 cm). Musée des Beaux-Arts, Pau, France.

PAGE 48 *[Self-Portrait in Library (Hand to Chin)]*, probably 1895, Edgar Degas (French, Paris 1834–1917 Paris). Gelatin silver print. Image: 2⁵⁄₁₆ × 3⁷⁄₁₆ in (5.8 × 8.7 cm), Mount: 5⅞ × 4¾ in (15 × 12 cm). Bequest of Robert Shapazian, 2010. 2010.457.4b.

ACKNOWLEDGMENTS

Thank you to my editor, Howard Reeves, for inviting me to do this beautiful book and working closely with me. At Abrams, I also thank the amazing designers, Julia Marvel and Shawn Dahl; Howard's capable assistant, Emily Daluga; and Marie Oishi, our skillful managing editor.

I am deeply grateful to The Metropolitan Museum of Art for collaborating with me on this project, with special thanks to Elizabeth Stoneman. The Met was the museum I most loved as a child.

I greatly appreciate the assistance of my agent, Elizabeth Bewley. And, as always, I thank my writing friends at Lunch Bunch for their encouraging critiques and support.

Susan Goldman Rubin
Malibu, California

The Little Fourteen-Year-Old Dancer,
modeled ca. 1880, cast 1922, tutu 2018.

SEE ALTERNATE VIEW, PAGE 36

INDEX

Note: Page numbers in *italics* refer to illustrations.

Dancer in Green, ca. 1883.
SEE DETAIL, PAGE 31